Happy Reading!

CIXI
"THE DRAGON EMPRESS"

By Natasha Yim | Illustrated by Peter Malone

goosebottombooks

Series editor **Shirin Yim Bridges**

Editor **Amy Novesky**

Copy editor **Jennifer Fry**

Editorial assistant **Ann Edwards**

Book design **Jay Mladjenovic**

Typeset in Trajan, Ringbearer, Volkswagen, and Gill Sans

Illustrations rendered in gouache

Manufactured in Singapore

Library of Congress Control Number: 2011924357

ISBN: 978-0-9834256-5-6

First Edition 10 9 8 7 6 5 4 3 2 1

Goosebottom Books LLC

710 Portofino Lane, Foster City, CA 94404

www.goosebottombooks.com

The Thinking Girl's Treasury of Dastardly Dames

CLEOPATRA
"SERPENT OF THE NILE"

AGRIPPINA
"ATROCIOUS AND FEROCIOUS"

MARY TUDOR
"BLOODY MARY"

CATHERINE DE' MEDICI
"THE BLACK QUEEN"

MARIE ANTOINETTE
"MADAME DEFICIT"

CIXI
"THE DRAGON EMPRESS"

To Tiegan, Alena, and Quinn, for being my loyal first readers and for always inspiring me. And to Brian, for his endless love and support. ~ **Natasha Yim**

"The Dragon Empress"

From behind the silk curtains of her palanquin, the last empress of China surveyed the scene. Exquisite palaces were charred, some burnt almost to the ground. Manuscripts and books from the imperial library littered the courtyards. Shattered porcelain vases, gold Buddha statuettes, jade ornaments, and other treasures lay scattered in the looters' rush to grab objects of even greater value. Foreign powers had not only penetrated China's defenses, but the inner sanctum of the Forbidden City. Cloistered within its thirty-foot walls, Cixi had lived a pampered life while her people starved. Her extravagant lifestyle, displays of bad temper, and brutal punishments on those who opposed her earned her the nickname, the Dragon Empress. Yet despite the fearsome name, Cixi could not keep the foreign nations out of China. Now, her palace and her dynasty lay in ruins.

Where she lived

Cixi was born in Shanxi province.

In Cixi's day, Beijing was called Peking. The Forbidden City, where the emperor and his court lived, was located here.

Cixi and her court fled to Xian during the Boxer Rebellion of 1900. They stayed for fourteen months. It was the first time Cixi had been in the interior of the empire.

Cixi most likely spent her childhood in Anhui province. Her father was an official here.

When she lived

This timeline shows when the Dastardly Dames were born.

69 BC	15 AD	1516 AD	1519 AD	1755 AD	1835 AD
Cleopatra	Agrippina	Mary Tudor	Catherine de' Medici	Marie Antoinette	Cixi

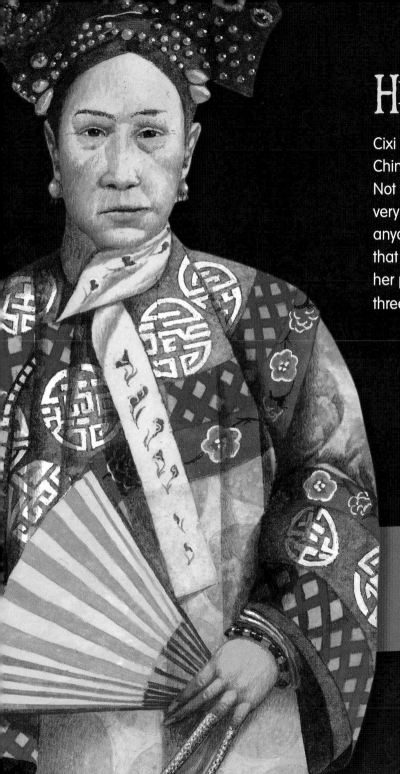

HER STORY

Cixi was born on November 29, 1835, in northern China, the daughter of a minor government official. Not much is known about her early life. Cixi was very secretive about her upbringing and would forbid anyone to ask her about it. But, she did once state that she did not have a happy childhood. She felt that her parents mistreated and ignored her while her three younger sisters got everything they wanted.

Yikes! It was the fashion for noble Manchu women to have six-inch fingernails on their fourth and little fingers! Cixi is seen here wearing filigree nail protectors. Rumor has it she gouged a manservant with her long nails when she flew into a rage.

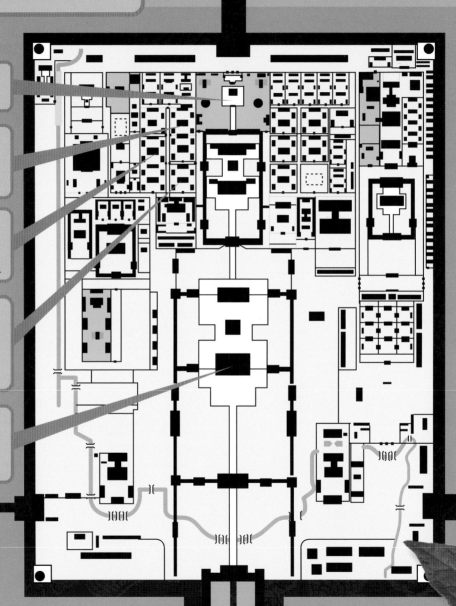

years, between 1420 and 1911.

Imperial Gardens—Members of the royal household came here to relax.

Palace of Gathered Elegance—First residence of Cixi when she entered the Forbidden City. Emperor Tongzhi was born here.

Palace of Eternal Spring— When Tongzhi grew up and moved out of his mother's home, Cixi moved here where she lived for the next ten years.

Palace of Eternal Longevity— When she was sixty, Cixi moved to a West Chamber in this building. The emperor and his wives were required to come here to pay their respects to her every morning.

Hall of Supreme Harmony— During the Qing Dynasty, emperors held banquets and ceremonies and met with foreign officials here.

When she was fourteen, Cixi's mother registered her for service at the imperial court. Girls between the ages of thirteen and sixteen were required to put their names in a book from which they would be chosen to work as either handmaidens at the palace, or as concubines—official girlfriends or mistresses—for the emperor. They were examined for physical defects and tested on conversational skills, grace, and other womanly qualities. Not everyone considered this an honor as, often, daughters never saw their parents again. One mother even sent her daughter to the selection process dirty, with tangled and uncombed hair, so that she would not be chosen. Cixi, on the other hand, considered this an opportunity to escape her miserable childhood.

It must have seemed like a wondrous escape when, at sixteen, Cixi was chosen as a concubine and entered the Forbidden City on a red, covered palanquin. Imagine her awe as she glimpsed the impressive compound of dazzling lakes, courtyards, and red-tiled pagodas, and breathed in the sweet-smelling scent of honeysuckle, jasmine, pomegranate, and other fruit trees.

In the sophisticated world of the imperial court, Cixi now wore beautiful necklaces of honey-yellow amber and turquoise silk gowns woven with patterns of dragons and the Chinese characters for "blessing" and "longevity." She made up her face with heavy white powder, marking the center of her lower lip with a single red dot.

Cixi led a fairly quiet life, amusing herself with her favorite Pekinese dogs, and taking leisurely strolls amidst persimmon trees and cherry blossoms. She waited on Empress Ci'An, the highest-ranking woman in the court, watched Chinese opera, and played cards. She gossiped with other concubines, embroidered, and studied poetry, calligraphy, and painting. In this way, Cixi was lucky, as elsewhere in China girls did not get educated at all. Nobody suspected that she would one day rule the country or be known as the woman who brought a dynasty crashing to its knees.

With 3,000 royal concubines, it's a wonder that the emperor ever noticed Cixi. Some said her melodic singing captivated him. In any case, she secured her status at court when she gave birth to the emperor's only son, Zaichun, in 1856. Cixi quickly moved up from concubine to Imperial Consort, one of the emperor's highest-ranking wives.

Cixi was actually quite an accomplished artist. This traditional Chinese scroll painting is one of hers!

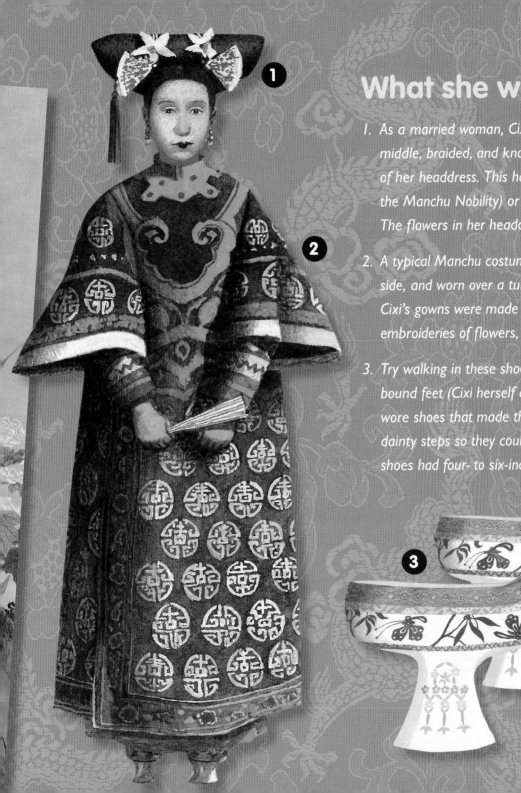

What she wore

1. As a married woman, Cixi wore her hair parted in the middle, braided, and knotted into a bun to form the base of her headdress. This hairstyle is called the Qitou (Hair of the Manchu Nobility) or the Jingtou (Hair of the Capital). The flowers in her headdress were made of jade or pearls.

2. A typical Manchu costume was loose, fastened at the side, and worn over a tunic or camisole and pantaloons. Cixi's gowns were made of silk or satin with intricate embroideries of flowers, animals, and emblems.

3. Try walking in these shoes! Manchu women did not have bound feet (Cixi herself detested the custom), but they wore shoes that made them walk with the same tiny, dainty steps so they could fit in to Chinese society. The shoes had four- to six-inch-high central wedged heels.

When Emperor Xianfeng fell gravely ill, Cixi suddenly found herself thrust into political intrigues far beyond her experience. She had to rely on her instinct and cunning. According to the custom of the Qing (pronounced Ching) Dynasty Emperors, the throne was not automatically passed on to the eldest son. The emperor selected his successor by writing his name on a piece of paper and placing it in a secret box. Upon the emperor's death, the box was opened, and the new emperor announced.

As Emperor Xianfeng lay dying, Cixi paced her room in a state of panic. Xianfeng had not yet put a name in the secret box. What would happen if he died without naming their son his heir? As merely the widow of a dead emperor, Cixi would lose her standing and prestige at court, but as the mother of a reigning emperor, she would have the respect and honor she wanted.

With her five-year-old son in her arms, Cixi burst into Emperor Xianfeng's room and held Zaichun up to his father. She demanded to know if their son would be his heir. Xianfeng weakly nodded his consent, and designated Cixi and Empress Ci'An as the young emperor's co-regents.

A throne in the Imperial City with a screen like the ones that Cixi used to hide behind

This outraged the emperor's Grand Chancellors. Women had not been in charge of the country since Empress Wu of the Tang Dynasty 1,000 years before! And they weren't about to let that happen again if they could help it. They claimed that Xianfeng had named them advisors to the next emperor before Cixi so rudely barged in. It was obvious the Grand Chancellors were not about to give in so easily.

Cixi acted fast! Before her husband was even buried, she arrested the chancellors and seized power by force. She beheaded one of them, allowed two to commit suicide (this supposedly showed mercy and respect for their rank as imperial princes), and banished the others.

Cixi renamed her son Emperor Tongzhi, which means "to restore together a state of order." She gave herself and Empress Ci'An the lofty titles of Dowager Empresses, and issued an imperial edict on the five-year-old emperor's behalf naming herself and Ci'An full decision makers, "without interference." However, as a woman in the Qing Dynasty, she could not be seen as governing. Instead, she gave orders from a chair behind the emperor, shielded by a yellow silk screen. She then had to make it appear that the emperor's advisors were really the ones in charge by saying, "I leave it to you."

The imperial portrait of Emperor Tongzhi.

Unlike her co-regent, Ci'An, who was, by all accounts, gentle in nature and content to take a back seat in politics, Cixi was strong-willed, ambitious, and easy to offend. She flew into terrible rages, sometimes gouging servants with her six-inch long fingernails—a Manchu fashion statement for noblewomen. She ordered those who displeased her to be whipped on the bottom with a bamboo cane like disobedient children. She had a reporter beaten to death for criticizing her. Once, so the story goes, Cixi even demanded that two maids slap each other's faces harder and harder in front of her. She instilled such fear that when the servant who usually fixed her hair in the mornings fell ill, his replacement shook so much that he accidentally pulled two hairs out of her head.

"Put them back!" Cixi shrieked. "Put them back at once!"

Even in quieter moments, Cixi was not very considerate of those around her. An attendant once said that it was characteristic of her to experience a keen sense of enjoyment at the troubles of others. She relished standing in the rain for hours, sheltered by a broad umbrella, while her servants and handmaidens stood out in the open, shivering and soaked to the skin.

What she ate

Cixi sometimes liked to order 150 dishes for imperial meals. It took 200 chefs and servants to prepare them! Out of all these choices, she would only select a few that were her favorites. Often, the dishes she didn't touch got recycled to the next meal. Sometimes, they sat around for days until weevils (a kind of beetle) crawled in them. It is said that Cixi liked to occasionally reward a favored lady-in-waiting with a taste from the royal meal. However, true to her dastardly nature, she never offered any food from her favorite dishes, so her handmaiden might get a sample of weevil-infested food, which she had to accept with a gracious smile! In each dish was placed a silver poison-testing plate, which was believed to turn black if poison was present.

Cixi enjoyed venison and mutton in the winter, and chicken, duck, pheasant, and mushrooms in the spring and summer. She also liked pork, especially the rind cut into tiny pieces and fried. Her breakfast usually included lotus root porridge and a bowl of hot milk sweetened with honey and almonds. Beans were an important part of Cixi's diet. She ate a lot of tofu or bean curd (made from soybeans), red beans used in glutinous rice balls, and mooncakes.

Cixi's favorite drink, douzhi, was a fermented beverage made from ground soybeans. She also liked her tea flavored with flowers such as honeysuckle, roses, jasmine, and chrysanthemums.

A portrait of Emperor Tongzhi, showing him as he rarely was: at his desk!

As a regent, Cixi's most difficult challenge was Emperor Tongzhi himself. The young emperor was not the son his mother had hoped for. Cixi once lamented, "I was lucky in giving birth to a son. But after that, I had very bad luck." Tongzhi did not care for education, reading, or politics. He preferred the company of his concubines, drinking, and smoking opium—a powerful drug—and sneaking out of the Forbidden City to enjoy Peking's rowdy nightlife. Some say that Cixi did not discourage this because it left her in charge.

At the age of fifteen, Tongzhi married Princess Alute, a nobleman's daughter. Cixi and Alute apparently did not get along. The young girl's spirited and outspoken nature threatened Cixi's influence with her son. Two years later, Tongzhi officially no longer needed a regent, as emperors of the Qing Dynasty could rule on their own at seventeen. Cixi retired to the Summer Palace six miles away. However, Tongzhi's reign was short-lived. When the nineteen-year-old emperor died of smallpox, Cixi was called back to the Forbidden City. Some even said that Cixi infected one of her son's handkerchiefs with the smallpox virus so that she could regain power. Alute's untimely death from an overdose of opium soon after gave rise to more sinister rumors that Cixi had poisoned her.

Once again, the reigning emperor had died without putting the name of his successor into the secret box. According to tradition, an emperor could not be succeeded by someone in his own generation or before him, such as an uncle, brother, or cousin; he must pass the throne on to someone in the next generation, like a son or nephew. The imperial princes, Tongzhi's uncles, all wanted to name someone from their own family as the next Emperor of China.

Cixi then made a bold move. She announced that she was adopting her three-year-old nephew, Zaitien, as her son, and declared him emperor. She had him whisked out of his family home and brought to the Forbidden City, a frightened, befuddled little boy. As Zaitien was Tongzhi's cousin, this was against tradition. However, Cixi simply bent the rules to fit her agenda.

A very young Guangxu trying to have some fun in the Imperial Palace.

A postcard of the Emperor Guangxu. This was a tinted photograph of the young emperor, and must have seemed very modern and Western at the time.

Cixi named Zaitien, Emperor Guangxu, meaning "Glorious Succession." Perhaps because she had lost control of her own son at a young age, she treated Guangxu more severely. Cixi selected his tutor, kept him under her ever-watchful eye, and by some accounts, was very harsh with him. Some even said she forced the emperor to kneel before her and eat out of her hands. Guangxu was prone to nightmares, plagued by frequent illnesses, and absolutely terrified of Cixi. He might have found a more sympathetic ear with the Empress Ci'An, which may have made Cixi jealous. Ci'An's sudden death in 1881 after a brief illness ignited further rumors that Cixi had again poisoned a rival.

A traditional portrait of Empress Ci'An. You can tell that she is an empress because she is wearing yellow, the imperial color of China.

When Guangxu turned seventeen, and was able to rule on his own, Cixi's role as regent again officially ended. She retreated back to the Summer Palace. But she had no intention of giving up power completely, and it's believed that she took one of the Great Seals, official stamps used by the rulers of China, so that no orders could be issued without her consent.

Guangxu felt it was time to modernize the country. He ordered the building of railroads and the improvement of the military, abolished useless government offices, and fired corrupt officials. He wanted to reform the legal system and restructure the civil exams for ministers. He became the first Emperor of China to read the Bible and learn English. Western ideas fascinated Guangxu, and he yearned to learn more.

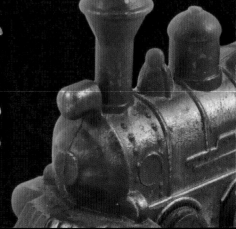

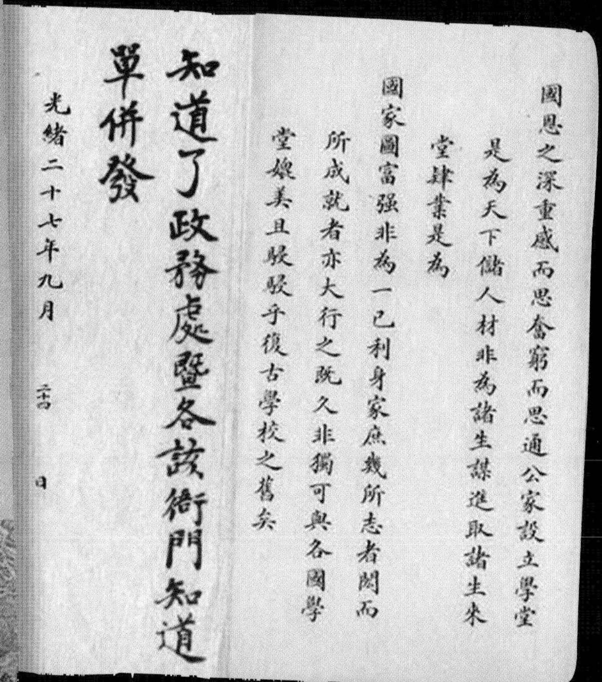

國恩之深重感而思奮窮而思通公家設立學堂
是為天下儲人材非為諸生謀進取諸生朱
堂肄業是為
國家圖富強非為一己利身家庶所志者闊而
所成就者亦大行之既久非獨可與各國而
堂娩美且股股於復古學校之舊矣

知道了政務處暨各該衙門知道
單併發

光緒二十七年九月 吾 日

Emperor Guangxu's imperial portrait, and his endorsement, in red, on Shandong University's charter. Establishing universities was part of his plans for reform.

Cixi, on the other hand, was very suspicious of Western ideas and felt they corrupted the Chinese way of life. She wanted to keep China the way it had been for thousands of years and was afraid Western ideas would change that. She fought against the construction of a railroad to Peking because she feared it would make it easier for foreigners to enter the capital. When an advisor convinced her to allow the building of the railroad, she decreed that the rail cars could only be pulled by horses, not by steam engines.

Cixi had had enough of Guangxu's sweeping reforms. One night, she went to the emperor, slapped him with her fan, and hustled him out of his palace like a common criminal. She put him under guard in Ocean Terrace, a palace in the middle of a lake. Some say that when Guangxu saw Cixi coming, he was so frightened he threw himself down at her feet. Cixi had some of his loyal aides and servants executed and replaced the rest with her own people. Not even Guangxu's favorite concubine, the Pearl Concubine, was allowed to keep him company.

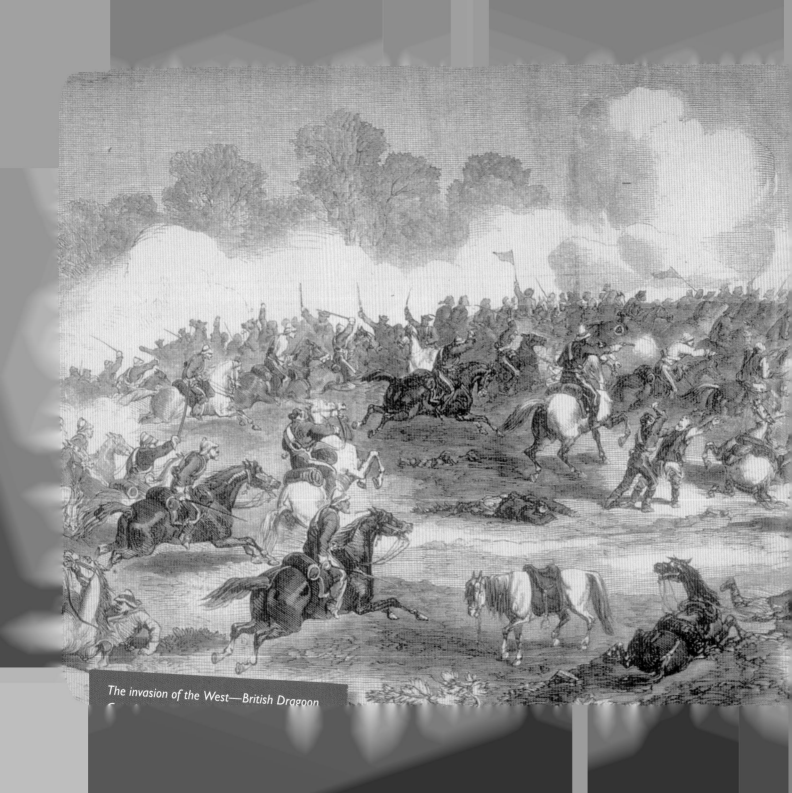

The invasion of the West—British Dragoon

Meanwhile, after losing wars with France and Japan, China had to give away a lot of land, money, and power. People accused Cixi of weakening the navy by using navy funds to rebuild her Summer Palace. But that's not all. Her lavish lifestyle—ordering hundreds of dishes to be served at every meal, requiring hundreds of bolts of silks and satins each year to make her gowns, and amassing thousands of boxes of jewelry—was impoverishing her empire and its people.

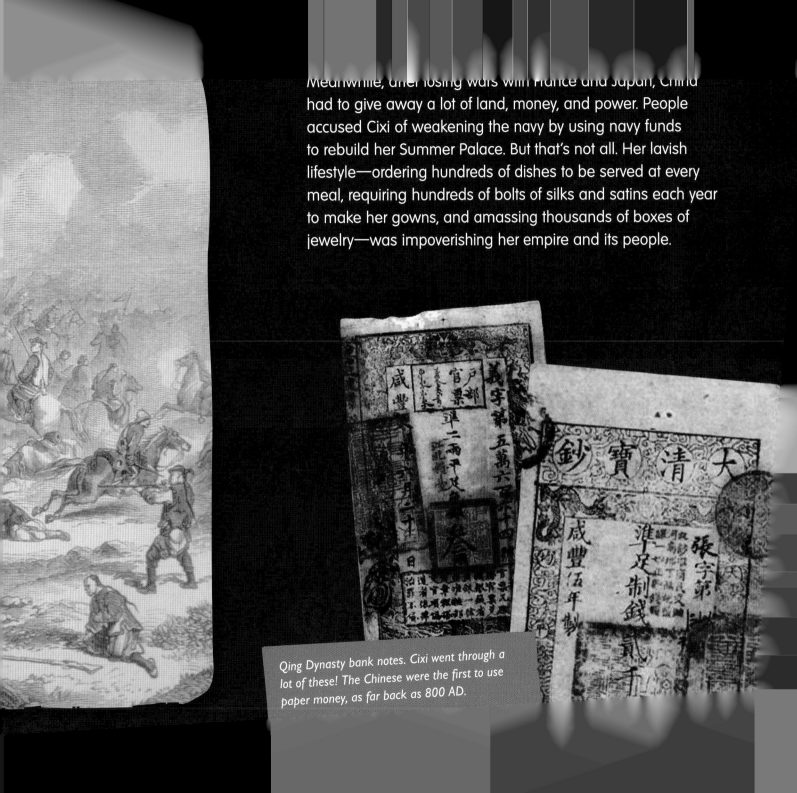

Qing Dynasty bank notes. Cixi went through a lot of these! The Chinese were the first to use paper money, as far back as 800 AD.

Peasant uprisings such as the Boxer Rebellion added to Cixi's troubles. The rebels burned churches and killed missionaries and Christian converts. When they also killed some foreigners, it gave the Western nations an excuse to launch an attack. Eight foreign powers sent their armies into China. Cixi and her court fled 500 miles west to Xian, deep in the interior of the empire. Escorted by 3,000 troops, the elderly dowager empress jostled about in a sedan chair, while oxcarts piled high with imperial luxuries and valuables trundled over bumpy and rugged terrain. It was a torturous trek that took two months. According to some, the Pearl Concubine begged the emperor to stay in Peking and face the "barbarians." Cixi, outraged by her interference, is said to have ordered her thrown down a well.

珍妃井

珍妃是光绪帝的宠妃，她同情井支持光绪帝的变法维新的主张，慈禧太后扼杀戊戌变法后，光绪帝被囚禁在瀛台，珍妃则打入冷宫。1900年八国联军进攻北京时，慈禧仓皇出逃，行前命太监崔玉贵将珍妃推入井中淹死。次年后打捞出遗体葬于西直门外，1913年移葬清西陵之崇陵（光绪帝陵）妃园寝。后人重新制作井口，不再使用。

The Well of Concubine Zhen

Concubine Zhen was the beloved concubine of Emperor Guangxu. She sympathized with and supported the Emperor's views on constitutional reform and modernization. After the reform was suppressed by Empress Dowager Cixi, the Emperor was taken into custody in Yingtai while the Concubine was confined in houses under guards. When the Eight-Power Allied Forces attacked Beijing in 1900, Concubine zhen was thrown into and drowned in this Well by Eunuch Cui Yugui at the order of Cixi.

This photograph is commonly—but not conclusively—said to be the Pearl Concubine. You can still see the well that she was supposedly thrown down on the grounds of the Imperial Palace.

To secure peace, China had to give away more land, money, and power. But it was too late. By the time Cixi returned to Peking fourteen months later, the magnificent Forbidden City and the Summer Palace had been ransacked and looted. Cixi had wanted to keep the West out of China. In the end, despite her efforts, the West had forced its way in.

As Cixi gazed upon the crumbled and blackened walls of centuries-old pagodas and palaces, ancient scrolls and manuscripts left to drench and rot in the rain, and shattered remnants of priceless imperial treasures, she knew her world had collapsed. It was said that she never recovered from this latest disaster.

On November 14, 1908, Emperor Guangxu died at age thirty-seven. Cixi passed away just a day later at the age of seventy-two. People accused her of poisoning the emperor so he could not resume his plans for reform after her death. But by then, the Qing Dynasty had lost a lot of its power and influence. The Dragon Empress' inability to adapt to a changing world ultimately toppled a dynasty that had ruled the country for more than 260 years, and ended 5,000 years of imperial rule.

Ruins of the Old Summer Palace. Cixi was said to have diverted thirty million taels (a measure of weight, the silver tael weighed around forty grams) of silver from the navy into refurbishing this complex, and extending it to include the New Summer Palace. Both palaces were ransacked at the same time.

DASTARDLY DAME (OR) MISUNDERSTOOD EMPRESS?

Dastardly Dame	Misunderstood Empress
Poisoned Princess Alute	No evidence of this. Alute most likely committed suicide with an overdose of opium.
Poisoned Empress Ci'An	This accusation was not made until about sixty years after Cixi's death! It's highly unlikely, as Cixi was herself seriously ill and was bedridden with hepatitis at the time.
Stole navy funds to rebuild the Summer Palace— weakened the navy	Navy funds were controlled by the Admiralty Board. Cixi did not have access to these funds. Her brother-in-law, Prince Chun, was the one who took the funds to remodel the palace in order to get into her good graces.
Imprisoned Guangxu in a palace in the middle of a lake	According to biographer Sterling Seagraves, Guangxu was very ill, and had gone to the palace to recuperate. He was not a prisoner!
Harsh and cruel to Guangxu	Sterling Seagraves reports that Guangxu had good relations with his aunt and trusted her.
Ordered the Pearl Concubine thrown down a well	Cixi and her court had already flown the coop to Xian when the Pearl Concubine's body was found. Most likely she'd killed herself so she wouldn't be taken by the "barbarians."
Poisoned Emperor Guangxu	In 2008, five years of research and tests revealed that the clothes and hair of Guangxu contained levels of arsenic (a poison) 2,000 times higher than that of a normal person! It seems he was murdered. But by whom? Cixi was only one of three suspects. This mystery may remain unsolved.